TITHING YOUR FOOD
BY
MARGARET DANGERFIELD

PUBLISHED by PARABLES
Earthly Stories with a Heavenly Meaning

TITHING YOUR FOOD
Margaret Dangerfield

Published By Parables
January, 2019

All Rights Reserved. No part of this book may be reproduced or utilized in any form or by any means, electronic or mechanical, including photocopying, recording, or by any information storage and retrieval system, without permission in writing from the author.

> ISBN 978-1-945698-87-3
> Printed in the United States of America

Readers should be aware that Internet Web sites offered as citations and/or sources for further information may have been changed or disappeared between the time this was written and the time it is read.

TITHING YOUR FOOD
BY
MARGARET DANGERFIELD

PUBLISHED by PARABLES
Earthly Stories with a Heavenly Meaning

Table Of Contents

Chapter I:
Food Is a Drug   p. 9

Chapter II:
There is Always a Reason Why We Do What We Do   p. 13

Chapter III:
My Experience With Eating Disorders   p. 17

Chapter IV:
Family Background with Addictions   p. 21

Chapter V:
Siblings Struggling with Food and Alcohol   p. 27

Chapter VI:
Why Did I Eat?   p. 31

Chapter VII:
My First Experience of Rejection   p. 35

Chapter VIII:
Food Disorders   p. 47

Chapter IX:
My Over Eaters Prayer   p. 53

Chapter X:
Hidden Wounds   p. 57

Chapter XI:
How to Break the Power of the Enemy   p. 61

Final Chapter:
How Do We Say, "Good Bye to Yesterday?"   p. 71

Tithing Your Food

This title is an eye catcher isn't it? What does this mean "Tithing Your Food"?

I want to take this time and opportunity to give God the praise! I thank God for this opportunity to speak to the body of Christ, and share tools that will bring forth "Health-N-Healing and a Victorious Life".

This is the will of God for his children to live an "Abundant Life in every area of our Lives"! Praise God!

Margaret Dangerfield

Introduction
"A Cry for Help"

Praise God! It has taken me great courage to write this book. Like some of us, it is hard to admit that there is or was an "Addiction" in our lives. I cried out to God to "Save Me" and "Stop Me" from destroying myself with "Food"!

We live in a world that puts demands on us to "Pleasure Yourself" in many ways. What do you mean, you may ask, "Pleasure Yourself"? Many of us struggle with "ADDICTIONS" secretly, whether we want to admit it or not. We look to whatever we can use to comfort us or ease the pain of life.

My calling and purpose for writing this book is to help the body of Christ who deal with "Food Addiction", and to discover there is a way of escape from over eating, through "Tithing Your Food to God".

What! Give God some of my food! Tithing is just giving back to God, a "tenth" of whatever, God has blessed us with. You may be thinking, give God a tenth of my "Food"? Yes!

You will be surprised how difficult this might be, just as giving God a "tenth" of your income, is the same principle with your food.

To some, it is hard to give God a tenth of your income. God only asks for a tenth, which is very small compared to the world's pressure or demands upon us.

I really didn't know I was battling this "Demon of Addiction". This is what it really is, a spirit called "ADDICT". An addict always wants more, never has enough, and wants to devour! This spirit is on a mission to "Kill", "Steal", and eventually "Destroy" our lives.

"Food Addiction", is destroying the body of Christ! We don't have to drink or do drugs every day, but we do have to "Eat at least three to six small meals a day to be healthy or to "Live"!

We are destroying ourselves in what we are eating, and how much we are eating! We are killing ourselves with "Food". We are being taken over by this "Food Addict" which is destroying the body of Christ!

Addictive Personality

I was on my way to doing the same thing, until I cried out to God. "Please God", Help Me! To be honest, I had to come to reality with myself first, that I had an "Addictive Personality"! This was a mind blower, "Addictive", Me?

As a young woman, I never used any form of street drugs, such as "Marijuana", or harsh drugs as "Heroine" or "Pills", etc. It was so funny, I liked the song "I'm in love with Mary Jane". I thought the song writer was talking about a woman not "Reefer"! I was just that naïve. Thank God! I only drank with the ladies, what we called "Ladies Drinks", with the cherry or little umbrella, an occasional glass of wine or sometimes a beer.

God has always had his hand upon me. God would not allow me to go too far with anything. There were people in my life that were alcoholics, used drugs, but didn't allow me to use drugs or drink too much. Family members and friends would say, "You don't want this, don't give it to her"!

Coming from a background where drugs and alcohol could have been my "addiction", instead it was "food". I wanted to eat to get "High"! Yes, comfort foods substitutes drugs, pills, sex, or heavy drugs like cocaine or heroin. Truth be told, food would be the drug of choice to try and fill a void in my life.

Sometimes we can't recognize this disease at first, because we are taught as children to clean our plates. We see all around us to "Eat, Live, and Laugh". We often use food to hide our sadness, express our joy, or comfort those who are grieving at family gatherings whether happy or sad (weddings, funerals and other gatherings).

We must be "Honest" with ourselves it seems okay to "Over Eat", rather than use, alcohol, drugs or sex. We end up making food our comfort. Now we have cried out to God, "Lord Help Me"! When I began to cry out to God, I heard the Lord say to me, "Eat to Live, and don't "Live to Eat"!

There is a great difference my brothers and sisters! When you "Live to Eat" instead of learning how to "Eat to Live", then we take back control over our lives.

If you struggle with keeping your weight under control, or struggle with eating the right foods, you are "Living to Eat", and now you must learn the principle to "Eat to live". "Your cries have been heard and have been answered with "keys" to live and not die. These are "keys" you can live with when you read this book. "Praise God"!

If you are having medical problems that solely connect to "Food" which is the primary source to your medical condition especially the type of "Food" you are eating, this book is for you.

It is God's desire for us as His children in the body of Christ to live in "Divine Health and To Live the Best Life we can live. Many have not lived that abundant Life Jesus wants for us, because of "Food Addiction"!

Mark 7:27 explains that as a believer in Christ Jesus, as a child of God, healing is the children's bread".

"Divine Health" is the will of God! According to 3 John: 2; "Beloved, I pray that you may prosper in all things and be in health, just as your soul prospers." (NKJVSTUDY BIBLE). So, there is "Health—N—healing". Our Health is in our Healing!

Like our soul is important to God, so is our health. Health related issues relate back to what we eat or ingest daily.

I am not a "Nutritionist", but I am a Registered Nurse for over 30 years. I have learned and have witnessed what we are eating. Eating large portions is the leading cause to serious medical problems.

I was crying out to God on my knees to help me in this area of my life. God told me to "Eat to live", and Not "Live to Eat". I didn't know that I was living to eat, instead of eating to live. Living to, was my next "Food Fix" which helped to cover up my deep pain on the inside of me.

Like most of you that are reading this book, it is a struggle to make the right decision every day. We must learn to choose Life and not Death! We must "Decree and Declare" (Ps.118:17); "I shall not die, but live, "And declare the works of the LORD. The LORD has chastened me severely, but he has not given me over to death." (NKJV STUDY BIBLE).

Through this painful time in my life, God gave me a "Prayer" as I cried out to Him that day on my knees, hands shaking. I was led to write "The Over Eaters Prayer".

I will share this prayer with you later in the book. It is time to read this little tool, and let God show you in His word how to take back control over "Food" so that "You may "Eat to Live" and not Live to Eat"!

Margaret Dangerfield

CHAPTER 1:
"Food is a drug"

You may still be in denial like I was. I would ask myself, "Do I have a food addiction"? I am not addicted to "Food", or anything else, I just enjoy eating! What I really enjoy is, "Fellowship" and making people "Happy". I love to cook, and enjoy friends and family gatherings, and "Food" is one of the ways we try to do this, make people "Happy". This is what we do, "We Eat", fix a lot of food, especially the wrong foods, which are our, comfort foods.

When we put too much emphasis on "Food" and not on "Fellowship", we lose our true focus. We make all kinds of excuses why we eat too much. Some examples are, "I eat, because I don't drink or use drugs, or run around anymore, but I love to eat! So, are we having an intimate relationship with "Food" now? The answer is, yes!!

The body of Christ has substituted food for the sins of their past. Food is now their choice to pleasure themselves. It's okay to over eat we think, but over eating is a sin.

The Bible tells us gluttony is a sin in 1st Corinthians 6:9-10; "Do you not know that unrighteous will not inherit the kingdom of God? Do not be deceived; fornicators, nor idolaters, nor adulterers, homosexuals, nor sodomites, nor thieves, nor covetous, nor drunkards, nor revilers, nor extortioners will inherit the kingdom of God." (NKJV STUDY BIBLE).

Proverbs 23:1-2; "When you sit down to eat with a ruler, consider carefully what is before you; and put a knife to your throat if you are given to appetite" (NKJV STUDY BIBLE).

In other words, if you know the trick of the enemy is to get you to over eat, knife it, destroy that spirit of gluttony that's trying to destroy you!

Another trick of the enemy is when we go to an all you can eat, "Food Bar"; we get high or drunk with food. Sometimes people eat so much, until they want to vomit, or secretly they do!

It is embarrassing to see how we pile our plates, because we paid our money, and we can't afford to come out like this with the family too often. We teach our children to eat as much as they can too!

Proverbs 30:8-9 "Remove far from me falsehood and lying; give me neither poverty nor riches; feed me with the food that is needed for me, lest I be full and deny you and say, "Who is the LORD?" or lest I be poor and steal and profane the name of my God (English Standard Version). We must come out of denial to be on the way to be delivered. (ENGLISH STANDARD VERSION).

1 John 1:9-10 tells us, "If we confess our sins, He is faithful and just to forgive us our sins and to cleanse us from all unrighteousness. If we say we have not sinned, we make him a liar, and his word is not in us." (NKJV STUDY BIBLE).

We must first see or acknowledge that there is a problem. "Wake Up! Food is a drug! We just exchanged one "Addiction, Food, Alcohol, Pornography, Drugs, for another Addiction! This is what we do when we have an "Addictive" personality.

Like Alcohol or Drugs "Food" is used to numb the pain, or acts as a "filler" to try and fill the void we are experiencing in life. We will satisfy ourselves in any way to keep from surfacing what is really going on with us.

Food addiction makes you eat too much, when you feel "Happy" or "Sad", "Lonely", or "Afraid". Stuffing ourselves with food becomes our drug of choice, so we cannot fill the pain! What is so painful, we keep trying to prevent the pain we are feeling from surfacing.

Margaret Dangerfield

CHAPTER II:
There is always a Reason "Why we do, What We Do?

I was told by my Father as a child, "There is never an "Effect, without a Cause". I did not understand what he meant then, but I do today. There is a reason we do what we do, and why we do it.

In this book we will look at some of the reasons why we become "Food Addicts" or, any other Addict. We need to look deeper within ourselves, and deep in our past to discover the real reason why we are trying to use drugs, food, sex, alcohol, gambling, or even success, to cover up what is really bothering us, or causing the empty void, or hidden pain.

There is an empty void deep down on the inside. This void maybe called "Poor Self-Esteem", "Lack of Being Loved", "Rejection", Hatred, or there could have been some "Tragic Event" that happened to us as a child or as an adult.

Feeling unloved, or rejected, is one of the most painful emotions you can ever experience. Some children or adults have never experienced parental love. Some felt abandoned or have been misused. This is a deep void for any human being to fill!
As we draw close to God, we will learn that only Jesus can love us, and only his love for us can fill that void, whatever it maybe.

It is true, we don't have to drink, or use drugs, or live a promiscuous life-style, but we do have to eat at least three to four or sometimes six small meals a day to maintain a healthy and balanced life.

Unless we have been called by God to go on an extensive fast for so many days, we should eat on a regular basis three to six small meals a day.

Let's not fool ourselves, whatever we use in the place of God, who is the Master and Ruler over our soul, will become a small God in our lives. This could be food, drugs, sex, alcohol, gambling, or even trying manically to be successful.

When, or whatever, we allow to "Rule "or become "Master" over of us in the past, ruled us. Now, we are delivered from the "Old Master", and now have our "New Master ", JESUS the CHRIST!

Luke 16:13; "No servant can serve two masters; for either he will hate the one and love the other, or else he will be loyal to the one and despise the other. You cannot serve God and mammon." (New King James Study Bible).

Hear what God is saying to the "Body of Christ" in his word for his children to live a Divine and Abundant Life! Romans 6:16; "Do you not Know ye not, that to whom you present yourselves slaves to obey, you are that one's slave whom you obey; whether of sin leading to death, or of obedience leading to righteousness." (NKJV BIBLE STUDY). What we don't master, will master us? Our sin will take over us and eventually will destroy us.

Some sins are called "Generational Curses", but we have been free from every "Generational" "Curse or "Addiction! Through the shed blood of Jesus, that was shed on Calvary, destroyed every blood line curse or "Generational Curse" and we

Tithing Your Food

are now free! We are no longer under that power of bondage of the past sins of our "Fore-Fathers"! Praise God from whom all blessings flow!

I have heard people say, "I love Food", I "love to eat". I have heard others who were addicted to alcohol, drugs sex, gambling etc., say "I love to get High", I like the "Kick" or the Rush" that I get when I am "High". The "Enemy" tricks us to seek this "High", or "Euphoria" repeatedly.

Therefore, it is insanity to think this, which then leads to "Addiction" which leads eventually to death.

Even being a Sex "Addict" gives them a sense of wanting to be loved, or the so call "High" they get through living a promiscuous life style.

"Gambling" gives the gambler a false "High" or Rush". An alcoholic seeks the same "High" but lacks "Courage" and gets drunk instead.

The "Enemy" or the "Addiction" says "One more Fix", one more time. And the truth is it may be our last time or fix. Remember we are looking for that fix that will comfort us.

Remember, that voice you are listening to is the deceptive voice of "Addiction, and Your Flesh.
Like we had to trust God with our Tithes, we will learn to trust God with our "Food". We will learn to listen to the voice of the Holy Spirit. That small voice on the inside that is our helper and will help us if we let Him.

If we allow our "Helper" the Holy Spirit to help us, just be still for a moment, a second, and don't give in to our "Flesh or our "Addiction that is crying out with a loud voice, just be still and do nothing! Psalms 46:10; "Be still and know that I am God; I will be exalted among the nations, I will be exalted in the earth! (NKJV STUDY BIBLE).

John 10:10; "The thief does not come except to "Steal" and to "kill", and to "Destroy. I have come (Jesus Christ) that they may have life, and that they may have it more abundantly". (NKJV STUDY BIBLE).

Like drugs or alcohol. "Food" numbs the pain or acts as a "Filler" to try and fill in the void. Food, "Addiction" makes you eat when you feel happy, sad, lonely, or afraid.

All these "Feelings or "Emotions" make you want to stuff that pain you are experiencing at this time. We want to overeat to help hide what we are really feeling. It becomes our "Drug to help and hide the pain. Why do we want to "Stuff or Hide" it, what's really bothering us?

As we look deep inside, we will discover it's not "Food" we really want, it is the need to be "Comforted" to be "Accepted, not to be "Rejected" and most of all "Loved".Food becomes our "Comfort" we need doing this painful time in our life. 2 Corinthians 1:3-4; "Blessed be the God and Father of our Lord Jesus Christ, the Father of mercies and God of all comfort who comforts us in all affliction so that we will be able to comfort those who are in any affliction with the comfort with which we ourselves are comforted by God."(NKJV STUDY BIBLE).

This is the purpose for this book to encourage those who are suffering in this area of their lives, to learn tools to help you allow Jesus Christ our "Comforter to Comfort us. Amen!!

CHAPTER III:

"My Experience with "Eating Disorders"

One of my experiences as a Registered Nurse, I had an opportunity to work on a unit that dealt with, "Food Addictions", or "Eating Disorders". Some of the patients, were dealing with many eating disorders.

Some of the patients suffered from Anorexia by starving themselves. This sometimes led to their deaths. Bulimia is a disorder where you over eat, then you purge or empty out the food contents you ingested.

Binge eating was a common disorder in the unit. A person would eat until they were uncontrollable. Binge Eating is like going on a shopping spree, you eat until you drop, just eating!

What I have learned, we are really trying to cover or hide the pain or shame that we are deeply feeling or have experienced sometime in our past.

Sometimes the pain we are experiencing or have experienced will make us eat alone or hide. Food is now our "Friend". If we really want to tell the truth, and be set free, "Addictions" are small gods in our lives? Yes!

There are "Laws of God" for the children of God, and that is; Deuteronomy 5:7 "You shall have no other gods before me" (NKJV STUDY BIBLE).

I can hear the body of Christ crying out! Those who are hurting and struggling with "Addictions!" And God is crying out!

Isaiah 1: 18-19; "Come now let us 'reason together" "Though your sins are like scarlet, they shall be as white as snow, though they are red like crimson, they shall be as wool. If you are willing and obedient, you shall eat the good of the land". (NKJV STUDY BIBLE).).

Is this our problem like the children of Israel, we are so blessed that we are eating the good of the land and have made them gods in our lives?

God told the prophet Isaiah whose name means "The Lord has saved", "Speak to the children of Israel to come to him to repent of their sins".

God wanted them to repent so that he could wash them, make them clean, put away their sins before him, and before his eyes, and wanted them to cease from doing evil. That "Evil" God was trying to reason with them, and still is today; put away "Idolatry!"

If we confess that "Over Eating is our sin, then God can help us. If we do not look at this as a sin, then God cannot help to deliver us from this sin.

There is a danger when we forget God and put other gods before Him. What! Are you saying we are putting these gods before Him?

Like me that thought was repulsive! "I would never choose any god, or anything, or, anybody over God!

The question we should honestly ask ourselves, "Have we made the Addictions we are speaking about a small god? Are

"Drugs, Alcohol, Food, Money, Sex, are they the gods of this world?

Have we made our "stomachs and strong desire for food, alcohol, drugs, money, lust, and all manner of immoral life styles" to be our god in this "Era"?

Let me put it this way, do we turn to food, drugs, alcohol to be our joy, comfort, strong desire for immoral living, to take the place of God?

No! We would honestly answer this question without any hesitation. But let us be honest first with God, you can't fool Him, and then let us be honest with ourselves; we have lied long enough to ourselves which is killing us.

Who or, what do we turn to for protection, when we are hurting or in pain? (The Ghost Buster?) No!
What do we use to help ease the pain? Recreational or prescription drugs, alcohol, food, sex, or even people to comfort us? We have made these substitutes, to be false gods in our lives.

Matthew 11:28-30; "Come to 'Me, all you who labor and are heavy laden, and I will give you rest. Take my yoke (Not the yoke of Food, Drugs, Alcohol, Sex, striving to be Successful or Acceptance), and learn from me, for I am gentle and lowly in heart, and you will find rest for your souls.

"For My yoke is easy and my burden is light." (NKJV STUDYBIBLE). When we use false imitators, instead of turning to Jesus Christ, the "One and Only true God, the God that was crucified, and bore all our sins in his own body, who suffered for us, made us free from all sins, we are in bondage!

Jesus came, and he set us "Free"! "Let's give God his Praise! We Praise God from whom all blessings flow! It is true according to Gal. 3:13-14; "Christ hath redeemed us from the curse of the law, being made a curse for us; for it is written, cursed is everyone that hangeth on a tree" (NKJV STUDY BIBLE). Why do we need to crucify ourselves, when Jesus has done this for us? Was his death and pain and sorrow which he bore for us in vain? The answer is No!

We no longer acquire the sins of our Fathers, Mothers, or any other "Generational Curse" that was passed down to us, "Poor self-esteem", "Intimidation", to dictate to us!

I want us to remember God said, "He was a jealous God"! God does not want us to put, nor have any gods in our lives to try and take the place of Him.

CHAPTER IV:
Family Background with Addictions"

I thank God for my parents, Willie and Velmore Blackmon, (they are both with the Lord now). We were a blended family with a total nine children; five sisters and four brothers.

We never said, step child, or stepsister or stepbrother in our home, we were one family. Five of those siblings are now with the Lord. (Tommie, Willie Jr., George, Hazel, and Samuel).

We loved our parents, and each other, and our parents loved us. My parents worked low paying jobs to support their family. My Father worked construction work, and my Mother cleaned offices at night.

To be honest, my Mother was the one who had the steady income coming into our home which I believed was an underling key that turned my father to "alcohol".

My Father was a weekend drunk. He drank heavily on weekends and lived an "Adulterous" lifestyle with other women, but I knew he loved my Mother. Those women knew never to say anything to my Mother about my Father.

I remember as a child I heard this lady say, "I'm going to tell your wife, and my Dad said to her, "Don't you ever say anything to my wife, and don't come around here again."(She came from the neighborhood tavern where my Father frequently visited on weekends), I never saw her again.

My Father did not always have a steady income to support his family. It must have made him feel like he was not a man.

My Dad was a proud man, and always demanded respect. Yes, there was some dysfunction in our home. When my Dad was working, there were less arguing and drinking. But when my Father was out of work for long periods of time, he would drink, and he and my Mom would argue and fight more.

My Father worked many jobs to support his family. My Dad also worked as a Pullman for the railroad in the past as well.

Both my parents confessed Jesus as their Lord and Savior. They went to Church, but there were problems. The Bible was taught to us daily. My Dad fell short with women and alcohol. We loved our parents and they loved us.

My parents would often say, "God will make a way"! My Father was a Minister, a teacher of God's Holy word, but he refused to be ordained.

Some of my Fathers drinking buddies were ordain Ministers but had the same lifestyle as my Father. I would hear my Father say to them, when his "Preacher friends" would come over after church, "I'm not going to play with God", and he knew his lifestyle was not pleasing to God.

This saying, "I'm not going to play with God", was passed down to his children. "Don't play with God!! I believe my ministry was passed from my father. I am now an "Ordained Minister" of the Gospel of Jesus Christ, for over 20 years.

Ordained Ministers as I have stated, were frequent at our home talking to my Father. They were trying to get him to become an "Ordained Minister". They knew my Father knew the Bible. I would hear my Father say to them, "You all have more women in the church, and drink more liquor than 905 which was a liquor store in the neighborhood."

My Fathers "Addiction" was alcohol and women. My Dad struggled with theses demons, until he stopped drinking. He stopped one day and never drank again. He Re-Dedicated his life back to Christ, lived to serve God and died at the age of 89 years old.

He never went to rehab, or a AAA meeting. He just asked God to save him when he got so sick one time and promised God that if he would help him that he would not drink or run around again! Drinking almost took his life!

By the grace of God, he miraculously stopped!! I never saw my Father drink anything other than orange juice ever again! My Mother was beautiful but was overweight wearing a size 22-24. My Father was the drinker, my Mother seldom had a drink, only on certain occasions.

My Mother was a very good cook and so was my Dad. When my Father was not working, he cooked, and could he cook! My breakfast was fixed by my Father every morning, because my Mother worked nights and got home almost time for school.

My Mother used "Food" to cover her pain; this was her second marriage to and older man. My Mother and her sisters and husbands and children would gather weekly (always at one another's home). We ate well!

Cooking a lot of "Food and coming together was the "Happy" time in our lives. We were always at one of the Aunts and Uncles home, and everybody had a job. We cooked, made ice-cream, and set up for the picnics or yard parties we always had. It was great!

The Men were talking and drinking, the women cooking, and the children played games, and made homemade ice-cream! Even when someone died, it was a lot of "Food". I believe that is how my Mom dealt with her pain in her marriage and struggling to pick up the pieces when times were tough.

I used to think my Mother was weak, because she never confronted the women, she knew my Dad was sleeping with. Most of them lived in the same neighborhood. The lived right next door and around the corner! My dad was an eye catcher, I must admit! He was a well-dressed man!

My Father had wisdom, and many of our friends would just come and listen to him. Our boyfriends and my brother's girlfriends loved our parents, especially my Mom. The young men knew not to try anything with us because my Father did not play!

My Mother was always a lady and a Christian and would do anything for her worst enemy. She even did things for the women whom she knew were sleeping with her husband! She would say with a smile on her face, "Good evening ladies".

I wanted her to show these women she was not weak and would not put up with their deceit! She really was the strong one!

I thought she was "Beautiful" but in my mind, my Mother was overweight. Despite her size, my Mother was a well-dressed woman. Both our parents worked hard to keep a roof over our heads and my mother opened clothing accounts to dress us.

Now I know why she used food and jokes to ease her pain. She was a prankster and always made us laugh. All our friends and significant others loved my Mother, but they feared and respected my Father! You could not fool my Dad!

My Mother later lost the weight going from a size 22-24 down to 16. According to some of her pictures before she married my Dad, she wore a size 12-14.

Margaret Dangerfield

CHAPTER V:
"Siblings Struggling with Food and Alcohol"

"Addiction" is a learned behavior! My siblings drank, and some would secretly get high, but obesity was a problem too. My brother Willie Blackmon Jr., died from a massive heart attack, he weighed over 300 lbs.

He was a musician and a great dancer, very light on his feet. They called him "Earthquake" he could really shake things up when he played that piano or drums! My brother was very talented could dance, sing and play most instruments. My brother was also called Jr., or Fat!

"Earthquake" was a big guy who could bring the house down with playing the piano, drums singing, and dancing. My brother knew about the "Tussy Roll" and the "Belly" dancing before it became popular. (We loved him so much), he was teased most of his life because of his size from a child until his death.

My Mother told me he quit school because he was teased by teachers and classmates who wanted to touch his breast and called him a girl. He was made to feel ashamed, and they found out earlier in his childhood, he had a glandular problem.

Later it developed into an inoperable tumor on the brain at 40 years old. He was placed on a liquid diet, and lost 100lbs. This made him very sick and he felt he was being used as a Ginny pig.

His God given talents put him in the spot light. "Food became his best friend". People would bring him "Food" all the time! There were people in his life, took advantage of him. He wanted to be accepted and him wanting to be loved for who he was and not because of his size.

My brother JR., Earthquake, Fat, died of a massive heart attack after coming back home from the hospital and was told he had the flu.

I remember when he was once admitted to one of the hospitals. I worked as a nurse. The nurses did not want to clean him because he was so big. So, I cleaned him, when I saw that he had not been cleaned properly.

This made me mad and ashamed. I would tell my brother, "You clean your personal areas and I will clean and wash you up myself when I come back". He was my brother and I loved him. He was a handsome man just "overweight". He died in his late forties or early fifties.

No one talks about the loneliness he must have felt inside. Smiling on the outside but crying on the inside. People walking up to him feeling on him. Sometimes, I think about how he must have felt being ridiculed by some of his teachers and classmates on a regular basis.

They ran him away from getting a proper education. He was called fat, stupid, and other names. No matter what his talents were, he was not good enough in their eyes!

Obesity seems to run in my family, which caused some to die early. Another brother who was very attractive, was well built, road his motorcycle and active, ended up with health issues.

He gained weight, had a heart attack, was on dialysis and died in his early fifties from "Congestive Heart Failure". One of my nieces died in her forties, she was overweight, diabetic, a suffered from kidney failure. Even though she had lost 100 lbs. before her death the stress on her body was too much.

My family suffered more from the effects from "Food" than alcohol or drugs. That it is why we must come against any strong holds over our family history or "Generational Curses! We must take control over our eating! We must say, "The Buck stops here! It's over!"

My, parents began to correct things in their lives that was destroying or could have destroyed them. We as Christians must do the same. We need to cry out to God and tell him, "Father you said you would perfect those things concerning me. "Help Me"!

Thank God my parents and aunts, uncles lived to be in their late 80's. They realized that "Food", wrong kinds of food, or, alcohol were destroying their families and their walk with God. Anything that controls you, have kept you in bondage.

Anything hidden, or you are ashamed of, has power over you. Deal with the "Cause and Effect", then, you will break the power of the enemy over you.

CHAPTER VI:
Why Did I Eat?

As a child I saw both parents struggle against someone telling them they were not good enough! They fought to survive, and against letting people put them in a certain class or box, called "Poverty".

They were proud people and wanted the best for their children. My Father told me when the reason kids called me "Black Margaret Blackmon", and teachers didn't want to choose me for a school parts was because I was not light enough, or pretty enough with long hair.

It wasn't because I was not smart enough in school but was "too black". There used to be a saying when I was a child growing up, "If you are White, you are alright, if you are "Brown", you can stick around, but if you are "Black" you must step back"!

My Father was one that really kept me strong enough to fight back with words. When I would come and tell my Father what the children would say about my "Fat" brother, and another brother who, had seizures, and I had to take care of him at school when he had a seizure, they would laugh. They would laugh at my brother, and that is why he dropped out of school and played hooky in empty buildings and smoked and drank.

They would call me, "Oh! Black Margaret Blackmon". For the most part, it was just those few children whom I later found out their homes were more unstable than mine!

They did not know the love and protection of a Father, and their life was ugly, so they wanted to make others feel ugly too!

My Father and my Mother seemed to know exactly what to tell me to survive and not be ashamed of whom, or what, at that time in my life. It was the love of God and my parents that helped me to be the woman I am today!

When someone tries to tell me or make me feel like I am not "good enough", I have learned to prove them wrong and God right!

Even living with some dysfunctions in the home, we were better off than some. Some were even envious the way we carried ourselves. Our parents were respected in our neighborhood, you did not mess with my Father's children! That's the way it was in our home, and in the community, "We were the Blackmon's"!

My parents made sure we were well dressed and went to church. Not any kind of young man could date us either, that was the rule with my Father and my brothers.

My brothers protected us from boys who my Father would say, "Good for nothing". They had to come to our house decent and not wearing "Kaki" pants or blue jeans. (Boy he would laugh at the dress code today)! My Father made sure we were treated like "A Lady".

You had to come to my Father and ask permission to see us and take us on dates. The neighborhood respected the "Blackmon's". My Dad would say to me, "The Blacker the Berry the Sweeter the Juice". My Dad would tell me, "Girl, you look like Clara Hurt and Lena Horn"! I did not know who these women were at that time in my life. But it was the way his face lit up when he called out their names. I knew they were somebody and must have been very beautiful!

This always made me hold my head up and stop crying, when I was teased about being dark. I found out later these women were beautiful and looked almost white! The way my Dad encouraged me, helped me to look good, and feel good about myself. Praise God!

My Dad loved all his children, but I was their baby, they had me in their older age. My Dad would keep me under close watch. I didn't understand it then, but I know now it was the calling on my life passed down from him to me to become a Minister of the Gospel.

My Mother would tell me with every challenge or struggle in my life, "If God did it for them "Who are they"? God will do it for you! Those words brought me through some rough and horrible times in my life. Even today, those words still echo in my ears to help me!

CHAPTER: VII
"My First Experience of Rejection"

As I think about rejection, poor self-esteem, I remember maybe at the age of seven-nine years old, was my first experience being outright rejected.

I was told by my parents, I was pretty, smart; and my Mother made sure I was clean and well dressed. I remember sitting at my desk with my legs crossed in school, this teacher came over to me and slapped my legs uncross, and looked at me with the most hurtful, evil, look and said, "Uncross your legs!

She made me feel like, "Who do you think you are, you are not pretty"! (I will later go in to more details about that day in the chapters that will follow).

I was so hurt and ashamed, the children laughed, and I could not understand why did she treat me that way? I was not unruly, running around or talking, why did she slap my legs uncross?

I was so hurt, I had on a real pretty dress, and I had been told I was pretty! It was so painful, I blocked out if the children were making fun of me, it was too embarrassing, and I felt alone and ashamed! WHY!

I learned to be well dressed from my parents. I heard my Father say on many occasions to me, "A well dress woman would catch any man's eye".

Even as a child it was very important to me to smell good and look good. I was afraid to tell my parents how this teacher treated me, because I thought I did something wrong! So, I cried deep on the inside why!

Trying not to cry in front of my schoolmates. That's when I learned to hide the pain, holding back the tears so no one would notice my pain!

Some of the teacher's would to say to me, "Margaret" you always look nice and smell so good". My Mother made sure of that, she always smelled good and looked nice even though she was overweight.

So, you see the importance of looking good and smelling good, became positive points I have held on to even today. I like to look nice and smell good!

I learned to master and hide my pain and true feelings. I could be sad but still smile. This is what led to overeating and trying to stuff my pain.

I now see my life could have been out of control even more than it was, before I cried out to God. Sometimes, you desperately want to be loved deep down on the inside; or accepted for who you are, and not try and be like anybody else.

When you see as a child, teachers be nice to the smartest girl, or the pretty girls and not you, you try and hide your pain, and seek to become people pleasers!

Sometimes you may fall in the hands of those who take advantage of those "Looking for Love" or wanting so bad to be accepted! I thank God every day for my parents. They were my backbone! When the world tried to tell me I wasn't good enough, they told me I was!

Tithing Your Food

Deep down, we want what our parents tried to protect us from, "The Bad Boys". God had a shield around me even from the "Bad Boys", you see they protected me!

It was the love of God and my family that kept me on the straight and narrow. The love of God kept me from the neighborhood sin, that was around us every day such as drugs and prostitution. The prostitutes would tell us to get away from around here baby, stay away from this corner go home.

The Drug dealers and Pimps knew my brothers and my "Daddy", and they would say you are that little "Blackmon", girl get away from around here! All of this was all around me, but God kept me! Praise God!

As a child, my father would save me a little beer when he asked me to throw his beer bottle away. My Dad's best friend let me taste some of his "Old Granddad 100% Proof whiskey. Thank God! It made me sick, from then on, I never liked the hard stuff!

As I grew older, I was always active in church. I loved to sing and recite scriptures from the Bible. This made my parents very proud of me. I was their "Good" little girl. I used to be always active, loved to dance, skate, play ball, and ride my bike. This kept me from being fat, so I was never teased of being fat, or ugly. I was still teased because I was too dark.

Another time I was in the seventh grade. I have always liked to dance, and there was a school part called, "Miss Spring Fest". I tried out for the part and was selected.

One of the teachers told another teacher, who was over the auditions, when she selected me for the part, she said, "Don't pick Margaret she is not "Pretty enough for that part".

That teacher wanted the "Light" little girl with long hair, who couldn't do all the dances. The teacher that stood up for me Ms. Turner, who is now with the Lord, fought for me and said, "Margaret is the right person for the part".

I was great that Saturday! My father walked (He walked everywhere) there to see me it was a long way from where we lived, and it was outside, and he heard the people give me a standing ovation!

I was so proud and felt so good inside, I couldn't wait to see the look on my parent's face, especially my Father, you see I was a "Daddy's Girl". It was through my parents who always helped me, to be my best no matter what people said or thought! I was great!!

I had so many positive people in my life outside of my immediate family. God had my neighbors look out for me encourage me to keep myself and go further than some of the children in our neighborhood. I was proud of where I came from!

Yet, there is always a snake lurking around to try to destroy the plans of God in your life. I was sexually molested as a child by a close friend's uncle. I knew better and should not have gone in that house looking for my friend when I did not see her Aunt.

We like to say, "Something told me not to go in there, but I was a child that wanted to play with my friend. My Daddy knew there was something about that man, and even some of his friends, whom they paid close attention too.

If you knew my Dad, my Father would have died for his children and everybody that knew my Dad knew that!

Tithing Your Food

Here again, I had been abused by an adult, and I didn't tell my parents because I thought it was my fault!

I was not to go in her house if I did not see her Aunt! If I had told my Father someone was going to die or go to jail that day! The man was going to die, and my Father was going to go to jail!

So, I never told anyone, but I never saw him again, he never came back over there again. He gave me money to keep quiet, and disappeared, this made me feel dirty!

I hated him and myself for that moment in my life for a long time. Smiling but crying, trying to cover up how I felt which was bad and dirty, that's when I believed, "Self-Hatred" entered. I felt dirty and did not like myself deep down on the inside. No one could see the little girl crying on the inside, because I learned to hide my pain and her at an early age.

When I graduated from High School and joined the United States Women Army Corps in 1965, I went to Fort McClellan Alabama for basic training. Upon graduating and finishing basic training, I came home on my first leave. My mother and I were talking, and she told me that my friend's uncle had died. I said it before I knew it, "Good" I am glad he is dead!

My Mother asked me why I would say such a thing! Then I told my Mother what had happened to me as a little girl. I had never spoken this to my parents about this man, and then she understood why I said what I said.

I had to forgive him from the grave later in life. I was at a women's retreat and we had to forgive those who had sexually, physically, or emotionally hurt us. So, I heard God speak in my spirit, "Forgive him from the grave! So, I said, I forgive you, for what you did to me and how you made me feel since that day.

I cried, and I went back, and I reached inside. I got that little girl and told her, deep down on the inside of me, "It wasn't your fought, you were a child, and did nothing wrong"!

I keep that little girl free with the word of God. "Therefore, if the Son makes you free, ye shall be free indeed". (John 8:36(NKJV STUDY BIBLE).

When I joined the Army, I heard someone, in the recruiting office say, "You came off 22nd and Franklin Avenue, deep in the Ghetto!" That was the first time I heard that, I came from the "Ghetto", and it embarrassed me I felt ashamed.

The people that loved and cared about me were "good people", not judged by where people struggled to survive! Now I use what they said about Jesus from Nazareth, "Can any good thing come out of Nazareth? Yes!

Something good did come from Nazareth! Our Lord and Savior Jesus Christ! And yes! Something good did come from 22nd and Franklin, "Me"!

Now I know that I am God's creation, and I am fearfully and wonderfully made by the hands of God! Praise You Jesus!

I was exposed to a one-time eating disorder, called "Bulimia". Throwing up after you have eaten too much is what the "Demon" makes you do! I was in the Army, feeling alone and here again not really dating anyone. I joined the Army, wanted to go to nursing school, so I could be somebody and make my parents proud of me.

I did not want to be promiscuous; it was all around me in there. We were young girls away from home, 18-19 and now thinking we were grown. Some of my friends took advantage of that.

My father told me then when I would call home, be a leader and not a follower. Follow the path God has for you, and that is "You are somebody". He was very proud of me.

My mother was afraid for her baby going away from home, but she was proud of me as well. My home training kept me from being "loose", but I longed deep down inside for that special someone too.

I remember the good things and the bad things that happened to me. I was taken advantage of by a soldier, but I did not tell because I felt ashamed. He was good looking and the women were all over him.

I felt, who would believe that he did this thing to me! I was not all that pretty, (You see, I had been told that in my past, so I learned to believe that). Why would he want to do this to "Me"! Back then you did not report this, especially on another soldier. "Forced or Rape"! Was a harsh word, he just took some is what they would say!

Still today, I can firmly say now, to all "Men", "When a woman or women say, "No!" "No" Means No! And if the truth be told, we still don't report it! It's not about looks, whether you are pretty or not, that people take advantage of you. Some men think that women don't really mean "No!

My problem was I was too trusting. I believed people were in general good. I was a soldier, and soldiers trusted another soldier! Sometimes this is dangerous, we must learn to listen to the signals or warnings the "Holy Spirit" is saying, "Something here is not right!"

He later apologized and thought I didn't mean No! Yeah, he knew he could have been court marshaled, dishonorably discharged! But I was ashamed and did not want anyone to know this happened to me!

One night I decided to eat a whole package of "Oreo Cookies. I did eat them, but I induced vomiting, which I later learned, this was called "Bulimia". I felt so bad, and ashamed of myself, I never did it again.

I could stop that which I thought would hurt or destroy me right then! I got that from my Dad. When my Dad said he would never drink again, he just stopped! I never had that urge to do that again, Thank God!

I experienced another disappointment. I joined the Army to become a nurse, not a cook! I was told when I joined the Army or back then known as The Women Army Corps, that I would be put on a waiting list for the nursing program. They made me a Cook!

I received most of my rank as a "Cook" in the Army, but deep down I was ashamed. It was so painful for me when I found out that most "Blacks" were cooks.

When I called home, I told my parents the recruiter lied. I was told that after Basic Training, I would go straight into nursing. That was the reason I joined the United States Army, to be a "Nurse", not a "Cook"! Don't get me wrong, that is an honorable profession. But I wanted to be a nurse.

My parents had a way of saying the right thing at the right time. They told me then, "Be the best "Cook" you can be until you get into the Nursing.

I became the "Head Cook", and then I went on to enter the Medical Field. Today, I am a Registered Nurse for over 30 years, Praise God!

Tithing Your Food

I fed the homeless in our Ministry and sheltered them for three years on a monthly basis. I thank God for my knowledge of preparing large quantities which helped to feed many souls.

Thank You Jesus! It is true; I've learned to take that which was so painful, and bitter, or sour in my life, and make "Lemonade". Praise God!!

It is true, "What the Devil meant for evil in my life, or in your life can become someday "Ministry"! Turn the "Lemon" or bitter experiences into "Lemonade" let God add his "Sweetener" which is His love into our lives.

Then we can tell others "Oh! "Taste" and see that the Lord is good! He is better than soup, "He is real, real, good!

In the Army, I would have been like a Medical Specialist, but after I was honorably discharged, I became an R.N.

I later married my first husband who was also my Army, pen-pal, and the "Bad Boy" from home. Eddie served almost nine years in the United State Army. When he came home, he was a heroin addict. He hid this from me until his discharge.

I married Eddie, he was strong (He is now with God rest his soul). But there was always this fear, that I would someday find him dead. He never used drugs around me. He protected me from anything or anybody and vowed to keep me and the children safe.

I became a widow at the age of 27 years old. I had two children and was pregnant with the third when he was murdered. I had this dream when I was pregnant with our last child.

I dreamt someone called me and told me in the dream he had been shot and was dead. His family and I found him murdered.

Thank God, he was not on drugs anymore. There were no drugs in his blood when he was found. Eddie decided to move away and stopped getting high before he passed. He left the old environment, got another job out of town, and came back for his family. Unfortunately, he was robbed and murdered.

This was a devastating time in my life. I was left with two children and was nine months pregnant with our last child together.

Here I had to go and find him that way with two little children and pregnant with the third! A month later I delivered our baby girl. I lost 17 lbs. during the end of that pregnancy.

My supervisor later told me I looked like I was, "Anorexic". I could not really eat, too much stress, during that time in my life. After going through that horrible experience, then my Dad died. As you already know My Dad was my world?

The strongest man and the one I could go to about anything and he would just say, "Keep on living", you will understand it later". My Mother would say God will make away!"

After being a widow for nine years, I met my now husband, "DeQuincy," whom I have been married to for 36 years. Praise God!

My husband "DeQuincy", (I call him "Honey"); God used him to help nurture me back and learn to love and trust again. We are both saved, and He and I have a son from this union together. We have raised our four children as one unified family. We don't use the word "Step" or half nothing, just Mom, and Dad.

Remember that teacher that gave me the part "Miss Spring Fest"? My husband and our children had the opportunity to hear that story again from this teacher. Years later, at the church we attended when I married my husband, DeQuincy.

Hearing her tell my husband and my children, how that other teacher did not want me to have the part, because she did not think I was pretty enough…. still brought tears to my eyes as she re-told the story.

She explained to them how she had to fight for that part for me! She hugged me and said, "Miss Spring Fest". I had never told anyone what the other teacher had said to her, but she said, "But I fought for Margaret, and she was the best "Miss Spring Fest" we ever had!!

I openly cried from the inside out this time, somebody understood how I felt and saw me and my worth to shine! Lonely, ashamed, keeping secrets deep down inside, will make you try and stuff those feelings.

You may even try to do things to be loved, putting yourself in harm's way to keep from feeling rejected. Inside of me was a little girl that needed to be set free, now she was!

CHAPTER VIII:
"Food Disorders"

I later became a R.N. and had the opportunity to work on an "Eating Disorder Unit. The first day I started to work there I heard the voice of God say to me, "I put you hear to learn". As I became familiar with some the different disorders, I realize that I had experienced some of the same behavior.

"Bulimia", "Anorexia", "Obsessive, Compulsive, Eating Disorder", that was me! The "eating when you feel "High" or "Low". I knew God put me here to learn, so I could help myself and the body of Christ.

We walk around like we are "Saved, Sanctified, and Filled with the Holy Ghost", and we are, but crying on the inside, God! Help me! Stop! Me from killing myself with food!

One of the things that I learned from working with patients with drugs and alcohol, whether its food, sexual abuse, shame or self-hatred, it is indebted deep inside.

We learn to well as children, "What happens in this house will stay in this house"! These hidden things will always have power over you! Anything that is hidden or covered up will rule you!

When that thing, whatever it is, when it is "Exposed" the power of that thing that once had you in bondage is broken over your life. There is nothing that is kept from the "Eyes" of God. God wants you delivered and Free!

One of the techniques, we learned on this unit while eating around the table, is called "Gentile Eating." While you are "Gently Eating" you will express why certain foods turn you off!

Sometimes people can't eat anything slimy because it reminds them of forced oral sex when they were abused as a child or young woman, or young man. Yes, men have been raped, forced to perform sexual acts in their childhood too. There is certain violence that is shut up in men, when men are exposed.

They feel like women as well, violated! Sometimes, men feel weak, and we know the old saying, "A real man is not weak but strong"! Well real men can't fight off five men when they are being violated, just like a person who has had a "Train" pulled on him, or her. This is what they called it when I was a young woman growing up. Let's call it what it is, gang rape.

How can anyone male or female, made to feel less than a human being feel strong? They have been left to feel less than anything or anybody!

This is how I help those who have been placed in similar situations. "It is not possible to fight off that many predators that violated you. You are a child of God, and your body may have been violated, but God has validated you as His very own and not man!"

It could be certain odors that would trigger certain hidden incidents in the past. One day I was really feeling good! I was on top of my game, on target with my patients they loved me; they said, "They liked when I was on, because I was "Real"!

This day, I was really feeling good about myself, I looked good and I felt very pretty, and I was sitting at the table, and I heard the voice of God say to me, "This is how you felt when your teacher came over and slapped your legs uncross.

She made you feel that you were not that pretty, and you had no "Right" to feel this way! (Pretty). For the first time in my life it was explained to me WHY!! Why did she do this to me? Because she felt "I had no "Right" to feel pretty and good about myself" she abused me.

But I do have a "Right" to feel or be who God says I am! Thank You Jesus! I am "Beautiful" inside and Out! And I have been "Washed and made whole through the "Blood" of Jesus! Hallelujah! Praise God!

I have now learned and still trying to master those feelings. To never allow anyone tell me I am not "pretty enough, or smart enough". Neither do they have a right to treat me any kind of way! I know who I am, and to whom I belong to! I stand on the word of God.

I often read Psalms 139:14;" I will praise you, for I am fearfully and wonderfully made: Marvelous are Your works; and that my soul knoweth very well." (NKJV STUDY BIBLE). This makes my heart smile.

Every accomplishment in my life, someone said, or tried to discourage me. Even those who were supposed to help me, were very negative. But God encourages his children that God is always with us. GOD always has a "Ram in the Bush to help us. "Hallelujah"!

When I think back, they may have meant it for evil, but God meant it for my good! God keeps proving He is "Big and Strong in my life.

Like my Mother used to say, "If God did it for them, (those who say you can't or will not make it), God will do it for you too! My Mother was telling me that God loved me like he loved them!

My husband DeQuincy, has been a great instrument in my life, and I, in his. We have learned in these 36 years of marriage, no one can love the other the way God can love us.

We must be willing to set the other free from trying to take the place of God like this in our marriages when we try to make people love us the only way God can love us, this is what causes crises in our marriages. We can't make him or her as idols in our lives! Only God can love us, fill those voids in our lives. God spoke to me and said, "No one can love you like I can".

God's love, and the way we need to be loved, is "Unconditional"! We should be aware of this; neither should we allow anybody or anything to fill areas in our lives that only God can fill! Not food, sex, drugs, or alcohol. Sometimes we can be in love with, "The idea of love, which is not real love"! We want people to love us when we can't love ourselves.

Wake Up! You must know God is "Love" and he loves "You", and God will teach us how to love yourself, and then we can reach out with the help of God and really love others, even if they disappoint us.

My Father loved me and my Mother. I was like Joseph in the Bible to my parents due to having me their older years. I was always treated special being their youngest child. When other people tried to tell me that I was nothing, I had to reach back and hear the echoes of their love in my ears and my heart. You see, I'm still learning through God the Father, to "Love and to "Forgive".

God spoke to me when I struggled to forgive someone who hurt me. "Margaret, it is not a hard thing it is a, "heart thing". I am learning that well. I have learned to love and trust God so much, it was through my Dad that I know God and love God.

I thought my "Daddy" loved me so much, and He would die to protect me, but Jesus my "Real Father, Dad, Daddy" did die for me to protect and save me. Praise God!

CHAPTER IX
"My Over Eaters Prayer"

My second marriage was ordained of God. My first marriage was mostly love and my flesh. "Eddie and I were soldiers. He was "Tall, Black and handsome". The bad boy from the neighborhood. We made the best of our marriage until his death.

In my current marriage, DeQuincy and I prayed together before we got married. We sought God if we were to get married (This is a wise thing to do), and God gave my husband the word. 1st. Thessalonians 5:18; "In everything give thanks; for this is the will of God in Christ Jesus concerning you". (KJV).

We knew this was a word from God telling us it was His will and approving our marriage. No matter what has happened in these 36 years of marriage, we always go back to this scripture and pray to be thankful, for this is God's will for us who belong to Christ Jesus."

Has this second marriage been perfect? No! I thought since we sought God, and we loved one another everything would be perfect. You see we dated in the past, before my first marriage. Our relationship did not last long, and we went our separate ways. We were not ready, but we found one another again. After being a widow for nine years, we fell in love and married.

We both thought this would be a story book marriage! The answer is in what I just said, "A story book". We were "Saved", there is no perfect marriage. The truth is, "There is no perfect person, saved or unsaved. We were a mark for the enemy to try and put asunder what God had joined together, because we loved God!

    We had to learn to fight the enemy together, and realize it was the enemy who works over time to tear down what God was building up! It was more than two people coming together in love, it was "Ministry". "Marriage is a "Ministry" and we had to learn to serve God first, then one another and our family.

    I have always known we were two people who had found a beautiful friendship. DeQuincy and I have always had one another's back! People don't like that! Now we have learned, to love God, self and then one another. Until you are rooted in the love of God, and know that God loves unconditionally, you will never know how to love yourself, and others. Halleluiah! Take a moment and let God love on you right now!

    We long for what only God can give us and that is "Perfect and "Unconditional love"! Release your spouse from that impossible task, that is God's pleasure, no one can take His place!

    We must learn to keep things and people in their proper perspective and hold on to our rightful position. God first, then one another, family, and Ministry if you are called.

    We make the mistake of trying to make people to be a small God in our lives. No one can love us like God. Nothing or no one can take His place in our lives.

    We had to learn to be submissive to God, then one another. My husband DeQuincy promised me years ago, if he ever married, I would be the woman that he would marry. "Praise God! He kept his promise! This was his first and by faith only marriage until death do us part!

Margaret Dangerfield

CHAPTER X:
"Hidden Wounds"

When a man and a woman get married, you don't see the "Hidden Wounds" that the "Tuxedo, and the beautiful "Wedding Gown" cover up.

DeQuincy had never been married. I became pregnant soon after we were married. He had an instant family. Within a year, he became a Father of four, and had a wife who had been called to "Preach". This was a "WOW" Moment in our lives.

My husband was a Special Education Teacher. He worked very hard for his family and for me to attend Seminary twice. It was hard at first, but we made it. People tried to tell us both that a woman should not "Preach", and his wife should not be a "Pastor" over her husband.

Therefore, I love my husband. It was my husband that told me, "Margaret you had better do what God told you to do, instead of worrying about what man is saying you should not do"! My husband had my back and our immediate family.

Even though God's hand was upon our marriage, we both had been wounded from past relationships, and we could not heal one another's wounds. When I realized that I could not heal his wounds from the past, and he couldn't heal mine, I began to cry out to God, "What's Wrong?

I was crying out to God on my knees. You see, I was a new wife, now a mother of four children, and called to "Preach" the Gospel of Jesus Christ! I was not perfect, he was not perfect, and we tried to make one another perfect, because we were called into Ministry and it was secretly destroying us.

We loved God, one another, we were saved, but we couldn't fill all the voids in our lives. We both suffered from past relationships and disappointments, and neither could heal me from pains from the past.

We were both wounded, hoping the other would love one another more than we loved ourselves. We both were hurting.

One day I cried out to God when that strong desire to stuff myself with food began to surface. "God"! What's wrong? Help Me"! This is the "Prayer" God gave me. My hands began to write". I call this prayer;

"The Over Eater's Prayer"

Father God, I Thank You for This Your Food; For the Nourishing of My Body.

I pray that I don't become a Victim of over eating today. But maintain being a Victor in this Area and Every Area of my Life. In Jesus Name Amen!

This prayer was given to me, Margaret Dangerfield, by God! I am the rightful owner of this prayer! God helped me with this prayer to keep "Food" in its place.

The prayer clearly states that, "Food is for the nourishing of our bodies", nothing else. Keep it in its place. "Food" is to nourish the body. We are no longer "Victims" anymore, we were in the past, but now we are "Victor's in Jesus name. Praise God!

No one or nothing can make you a "Victim" unless you let them. The prayer from God told me, "To maintain being a Victor in this area and every area of my life"! I am a "Victor"! As children of God we are "Victors", no longer "Victims"!

When I prayed this prayer, I did not over eat! Sometimes I did not want to pray this prayer because I still wanted to over eat! This prayer will work if you pray and mean it from your heart. If you pray this Prayer, it will work for you, so pray the Prayer and watch the power of God work for you!"

God gave me this prayer to help me first, and the body of Christ. I started teaching an "Over Eater's Group" in my home and with friends. Many have learned and are still learning to control their eating. Some have lost weight. This is an "Anointed Prayer", straight from the throne of God!

As I have confessed earlier, it worked for me then, and it still works for me now. The prayer helps me keep food under control in my life today.

I've learned that my loving husband, children, Ministry, close friends, can be very vital in my life, but can never take the place of God.

When we take off the Wedding dress and the Tux goes back, then we see two imperfect people trying to be the very best that they can be. We need to learn to accept them for who they are.

Our life is more stable. Our family is more stable and our children and grandchildren, are our main ministry. Our Ministry is about ministering to those who are hurting and need someone just to be real!

"For we seek the "Lost" at all Cost" is our mission! People need Jesus, and they are hurting in many of the areas I have discussed in this book.

It took a lot of courage to tell my testimony which my greatest joy is now to see others take control over their lives again. When we see people struggling every day in this area, we need to really pray for them to "Let Go" and Let God". Put things back in proper perspective in their life.

Romans 12:1-2 "I beseech you therefore, brethren, by the mercies of God, that you present your bodies a living sacrifice, holy, acceptable to God, which is your reasonable service. And do not be conformed to this world, but be transformed by the renewing of your mind, that you may prove what is that good and acceptable and perfect will of God." (NKJV STUDY BIBLE).

We must be renewed in our minds about food and allow God to be first in everything. Life is much easier when you learn to love God, and let God help you to "Forgive" those who hurt us.

CHAPTER XI:
"How to Break the Power of the Enemy"

When you learn "Hidden Things" has power over you, you will want to cry out to God to make you free, from shame, pain, rejection, self-hatred, and poor self-esteem. Remember you are free!

Anything that has been exposed, no longer has power over you! This book has been written, and I have exposed "Hidden Things". Truths about myself, things that were so painful, but have become my greatest ministry to help others, and defeat the enemy.

"Let God break this shame over your life that you will be free! Let God take away that shame! Isaiah 61:3 "To appoint unto them that mourn in Zion, to give them beauty for ashes, the oil of joy for mourning, the garment of praise for the spirit of heaviness, that they might be called trees of righteousness, the planting of the LORD, that he might be glorified"! (KJV).

Another way to break the power of the enemy with "food" is to use this tool! This is the most powerful tool to break that strong desire to "Over Eat", "Give God a "Tenth" of your food each time you eat! What! Give God a "Tenth" of my food?

If you are a "Tither with your money, start being a "Tither with your "Food". It will work if you keep God first. God requires the first of everything, it belongs to God! That means our money, ministries, children, because he gave himself to us first!

So, why not give God his portion first. Try this and see the salvation, deliverance of God in this area of your life as well!

This maybe hard at first, just like it was to discipline, my brothers and sisters" to "Tithe" your money. It takes discipline and this "Prayer "in this book will help you "Tithe" your food. We learn to be disciplined in bringing our "Tithes" to God, learn to be disciplined to give God and "Tithe" your food.

When you start "Tithing" your food, you will see God bless your 90% just like he blesses our money. He doesn't ask for much, just a "Tenth". If you will be honest with yourself, it was hard to put that "Tenth" aside just like at first it was hard to give a "Tenth" of our salary.

The more you do this little simple observance; this will help you break the power of gluttony. Remember, "Food" is only to nourish our bodies. If you can't give it up, you have given food too much power over you! It's just "Food"!

Get up from the table, set God's portion aside and go to the trash can and throw it away! Out of sight, out of mind!

Don't let the Devil still this most powerful tool and try and tell you this will not work! It will work and if you pray the "Over Eaters Prayer", you will always be victorious! Try It! Remember "Food" is just for nourishing our bodies! It has no power over you!

Here are some Warning signs! Be careful and take heed when we go to The All You Can Eat Food Bars? Use these tools:

1. Give God a "Tithe" of your food
2. Eat until your stomach says "Stop"!
3. Get up and walk away when you fill tempted to "Overeat"!
4. Don't become a "Victim" again!

5. Pray this Prayer?
6. Remember you are a "Victor:
7. Remember your goal is to "Eat to live" and Not Live to eat".
8. When you are struggling call somebody and tell them what "Really" is bothering you!
9. Remember what is "Hidden" has power over you!
10. Nothing and No one can take the place of God in your life! Food is not your God!!

As Christians we think its okay to "Over Eat". We serve God in the Church, in our various "Ministries", and then we go out and eat. That is our "Joy" our Happy Hour" in place of drugs and alcohol.

God told me it was not the food that I was seeking, but "Fellowship", and to be accepted. "The Ministry that people need today is the "Ministry" of Jesus Christ". The "Ministry" that teaches us how to "Love, "Forgive", and to "Encourage" one another every day of our lives, will bring forth "Koinonia", great fellowship".

We Need Deliverance! So, people can be set free! Those who have been called to help heal, we need a healing ourselves! Those who have been called to help encourage our brothers and our sisters in the vineyard, we need to be encouraged, to fight the "Good Fight of Faith.

I know my calling. Sure, I have received several degrees in Nursing, Biblical Studies, Ministry, and M.Div." I have taken classes to learn more about addictions, HIV and AIDS.

Our Ministry has supported those in the streets, in shelters, helped homeless families, prisons, taught in a Bible College, Youth ministry, Marriage Ministry and have been on three radio stations.

As an Airport Minister, we served three churches. I now have the pleasure of Pastoring Rose of Sharon Christian Fellowship Church/Outreach Ministries.

I believe God called me now to reach out to those that are struggling with obesity and food addiction in the Body of Christ. I have been called to share these tools with you who are crying out to God, "Lord help me not kill myself with Food"! I want to finish my course, and not let sickness or diseases stop me!

God calls imperfect people to prove Him to be "Merciful, Forgiving, and Strong, in the lives of those who makes him Lord over their lives. When I am weak, He is strong!

So, like my Dad, I don't ever want to play with God, for I take my calling from God seriously. I have exposed and shared the "Hidden" things that secretly made me have a strong desire to try and fill those empty and painful voids with "Food" in my life.

I thank God for deliverance from rejection and abuse. I was afraid and ashamed of these weights that made me want to be cleansed. People or anything can't cleanse you, only through the "Blood of Jesus you can be made whole. Thank you, Jesus!

The enemy would want me to be embarrassed and ashamed. I find that I am not alone, and I have set that little girl free through Christ Jesus who did not like herself for accepting the money and not telling her parents.

I can forgive that teacher making me feel not pretty. I can forgive that Nursing instructor that told me "White people have more "Grey Matter", (thinking power) and "Blacks didn't have enough when I was struggling to become an R.N.

I don't have to remember that old neighborhood saying, "If you are White you are alright, if you are Brown you can stick around, but if you are Black, you have to step back." Now the world is saying, "Black Girls Rock"! I say it loud today "I'm Black and I am Proud.

But most of all I say boldly what the word of God says about me and others that have experienced or, experiencing this right now in your life. Say what God says about you!

"I will praise you, for I am fearfully and wonderfully made; Marvelous are your works; and that my soul knows very well." (Psalms 139:14 (NKJV).

They call it "bulling" today, children are killing themselves and one another because they are not accepted by their peers. There is more going on in their lives than "Food" its "Pain"!

All that pain stuffed, then we try to purge ourselves by eliminating that which made us feel dirty, unclean, not pretty, not worthy of God. We try to rid ourselves of these bad experiences that happened in our lives. Thank God! We are learning "Why we do what we do"! Until you go "Deep" you will keep doing the same thing.

Those things we keep hid that made us ashamed or rejected, not feeling good about ourselves, no matter what happens or has happened, has power over you! When you expose the Devil and let God deliver you and get rid of the shame, then it will lead to true healing.

God tells us to eat in moderation, to eat until I was full and then push away from the table. I was very successful with the tools I learned from the unit. However, I found when around others I slipped and began overeating. I was hungry, angry, lonely, and very tired.

These are the triggers I learned as a Nurse working on a unit to help those dealing with drugs, alcohol, and eating disorders. The word "HALT"!

    H-Don't get too Hungry
    A-Don't get to Angry
    L-Don't get too Lonely
    T-Don't get to Tired.

When we are dealing with these strong emotions, they will trigger that strong desire to "Eat", "Drink", "Binge". Remember an Alcoholic should not hang with people who drink or be in bars. A Food Addict should not hang with those who hang at all you can eat food places. You will over eat or drink!

If I am in a situation like this on an outing, I pray the "Anointed Prayer before I eat.

Now the main tool, is to Tithe your Food to God to keep you from "Over Eating. This really is what this book is all about. "Tithing With your Food, gives Giving God a 10th of your food, and breaks the power of food over you"!

God always requires the first fruits of our labor. Remember, "Eat to Live" and not "Live to Eat". Give God His portion, and watch He will fill you with power, which is more than "Food". Praise God!

I had to set God's portion aside first! Just like we set God's Tithe aside first with our money! Give God his first portion of everything! Yes! Even your food.

Tithing Your Food

Tithing with your Food will work. Give God a tenth, then God takes our 90% which is left, and blesses it which is more than enough.

At first you find yourself wanting to take God's tenth and eat it. Look at it! It's just "Food" or its just "Money"! It's not ours its God's!

In this book the "Key's God has given us will help control our eating and help to restore our health"! Remember the "Over Eaters Prayer, "Food has to be kept in its place for the nourishing of our bodies"! Food is not a Fixer, Comforter, or neither can it take the place of God in our lives to fill the void.

Food and money are the hardest things to surrender to God, but it takes trusting in God to provide all our needs, for God is:

*1. Jehovah Elohay" The Lord MY God.
*2. God is "Jehovah JIREH"! The Lord My Provider.
*3. God is our "JEHOVAH ROPHE" The Lord MY Health.
*4. God is "JEHOVAH SHALOM" MY Peace and Wholeness".

The body cries to be comforted, when it is hurting, or when we are in pain, we try to hide the pain, stuff the pain, and not deal with the pain we are really feeling. We are ashamed to tell a friend I am hurting! I am smiling on the outside but crying on the inside! Not only do you eat when you are happy, sad, but when you are "angry, feeling excited, you want to "Celebrate!"

*Remember the prayers asked God to help us not to become a "Victim" today but maintain being a "Victor"! Not just in this area but maintain being a "Victor" in every area of our lives! Praise God!

We are "Victors" no longer "Victims". Let us stop playing the role of being a "Victim". SAY NO MORE!!! We must Move On! Christian Soldiers!

These are keys to help you depend more on God than yourself or anything that will try and take the place of God in your life. The "Food Addict" will try to trigger "Over Eating." The purpose of "Addiction" is to destroy us.

We must be like Joseph when temptation wants to destroy our relationship with God, we must RUN! Push away from the table, get up go in the bathroom to pray, drink more water; tell that "Demon" whom the son set free is free indeed! We are no longer in bondage to "Generational Demon's"! The curse is not on me, I have been set free through the "Blood" of the Lamb, JESUS THE CHRIST! John 8:36, "Therefore if the Son makes you free, you shall be free indeed".

Let us learn to let "Food" "work" for us, and we not work for "food". What I mean by this is, "Strip" the power "Food"" has over us and know that we have the power over food! "Let Go" of the control that put us in this helpless and hopeless condition.

When I am feeling weak, I am learning to, Wait, don't act on this action to indulge with food, Pray to God for His strength, listen to the Holy Spirit, and say with confidence, "This Too Shall Pass!

We see our brothers and sisters who are severely over weight struggling to live, walk and even talk. What we eat and the amount we are eating is killing us! We must not be drawn back into bondage with those things we used to hide our pain that once held us in bondage. Your ministry will help others be set free! Give it to Jesus and leave it there!

Tithing Your Food

- Remember the first sin was because of disobedience with food! That "Devil" the trickster is still sly and lurking around. You cannot out trick a trickster, but you can be obedient to the voice of God and live! Jesus came that we may live an abundant life free from bondage!

I remember when I was struggling with these principles, I Heard this in my spirit, "Have you applied the "Blood"?

God keeps me when I pray this prayer that I have shared with you. Then, I eat until I am full and get up and walk away. I give God a tenth of my food in what I consider the proper amount of food. Disciplining myself this way helps me to stay healthy! Yes, you must eat the healing foods, but Addictive "Personalities" will undue anything!

This is the goal for this book is to "Help the Body of Christ" with the tools I have learned and are actively using them in my everyday life. Not only will you take the power back over food, but you will even lose weight and be in the will of God for divine healing.

My doctor tells me keep doing what you are doing! This will only work if you work it. I heard this a lot dealing with alcohol, drugs, food or addiction programs. You must work the program that has been given to help you.

Remember you have chosen "Food" to be your drug of choice. Let's stop the insanity! We can do it! Praise God! There are too many people that can be helped or even delivered if we apply the tools in this book.

We will no longer let the sins of our Fore-Fathers, what my Daddy did, what my Mama did, or the sins of the world have power over us. That which is done in secret will hold you in bondage.

We can no longer give power to the bad things that may have happened to us to destroy our lives, but we must continue to "Fight the Good Fight of Faith".

FINAL CHAPTER
How do we say, "Good Bye to Yesterday"?

Don't let our past hurts, sorrows, disappointments, shame, rejections, hold us in bondage! It is time to bury those things that keep us in insanity.

Insanity is when you keep doing the same things expecting a different outcome! When we say good bye to our addictions, we grieve. It's like losing a friend, a loved one, it's a funeral, where we say good bye. You will experience a grieving, a letting go, but it is time to bury the "Addictions" in our lives, that appeared to be our "Friend" but really is our "Enemy"!

It's so hard to say goodbye to that which we have hung on to for so long! The Apostle Paul reminds us in Philippians 3:12-14; "Not that I have already attained, or am already perfected; but I press on, that I may lay hold of that for which Christ Jesus has also laid hold of me.

Brethren, I do not count myself to have apprehended, but one thing I do, forgetting those things which are behind and reaching forward to those things which are ahead, I press toward the goal for the prize of the upward call of God in Christ Jesus." (NKJV STUDY BIBLE).
Remember "Food" Is a Drug", don't overdose, which could lead to death, "Just Give It to God"! Amen! Praise God!!

ABOUT THE AUTHOR

Pastor Margaret Dangerfield resides in the St. Louis, MO. area. She is the Pastor of Rose of Sharon Christian Fellowship Church/Outreach Ministries. Pastor Dangerfield possesses a Master of Divinity Degree(M. Div.) from Eden Theological Seminary of Webster Grove MO. She also served in the United States Army and is a retired R. N. She is married to Minister Dequincy DangerfieldII and the proud mother of four children and eight grandchildren, 1 daughter in law and 2 son in laws. She has three living siblings; Ruth, Armelia and Cleotha. She would like to thank her family and mentors for their support. Praise God!

MY SCRIPTURES: TITHING YOUR FOOD

PSALM 46:10: NKJV STUDY BIBLE
PSALM 118:17-18 NKJS STUDY BIBLE
PSALM 139:14; NKJV STUDY BIBLE
3JOHN: 2 NKJV STUDY BIBLE
1CORINTHIANS 6: 9-10; NKJV STUDY BIBLE
PROVERBS 23: 1-2; NKJV STUDY BIBLE
PROVERBS 30: 8-9; ENGLIISH STANDARD VERSION
1JOHN 1: 9-10; NKJV STUDY BIBLE
LUKE 16: 13; NKJV STUDY BIBLE
ROMANS 6:16; NKJV STUDY BIBLE
ROMANS 12:1-2; NKJV STUDY BIBLE
JOHN 10:10; NKJV STUDY BIBLE
JOHN 8:36; NKJV STUDY BIBL
2CORINTHIANS 1:3-4; NKJV STUDY BIBLE
DEUTERONOMY 5:7 NKJV STUDY BIBLE
ISAIAH 1:18-19; NKJV STUDY BIBLE
ISAIAH 61:3; NKJV STUDY BIBLE
MATTHEW 11:28-30; NKJV STUDY BIBLE
1THESSALONIANS 5:18; NKJV STUDY BIBLE

Tithing Your Food

Margaret Dangerfield

www.ingramcontent.com/pod-product-compliance
Lightning Source LLC
Chambersburg PA
CBHW052103110526
44591CB00013B/2333